Learning Short-take®

STRATEGIC TRAINING MANAGEMENT

Transforming the business of training

CATHERINE MATTISKE

TPC - The Performance Company Pty Ltd
Level 20, Darling Park
Tower 2, 201 Sussex Street,
Sydney NSW 2000
Australia

ACN 077 455 273
email: tpc@tpc.net.au
Website: www.catherinemattiske.com

© TPC – The Performance Company Pty Limited
First edition published in 2006
Second edition published in 2011
Third edition published in 2022

All rights reserved. Apart from any fair dealing for the purposes of study, research or review, as permitted under Australian copyright law, no part of this publication may be reproduced by any means without the written permission of the copyright owner. Every effort has been made to obtain permission relating to information reproduced in this publication.

The information in this publication is based on the current state of commercial and industry practice, applicable legislation, general law and the general circumstances as at the date of publication. No person shall rely on any of the contents of this publication and the publisher and the author expressly exclude all liability for direct and indirect loss suffered by any person resulting in any way from the use of or reliance on this publication or any part of it. Any options and advice are offered solely in pursuance of the author's and the publisher's intention to provide information, and have not been specifically sought.

For eBook version: By payment of the required fees, you have been granted the non-exclusive, non-transferable right to access and read the text of this e-book on screen. No part of this text may be reproduced, transmitted, downloaded, decompiled, reverse engineered, or stored in or introduced into any information storage retrieval system, in any form or by any means, whether the electronic or mechanical, now known or hereinafter invented, without the express permission of the author.

A catalogue record for this book is available from the National Library of Australia

National Library of Australia
Cataloguing-in-Publication data

Mattiske, Catherine
Strategic Training Management: Transforming the business of training

ISBN 978-1-921547-32-4

1. Occupational training 2. Learning I. Title

370.113

Distributed by TPC - The Performance Company - www.catherinemattiske.com
For further information contact TPC - The Performance Company, Sydney Australia on +61 (02) 9555 1953.

HELLO.

Welcome to the Learning Short-take® process!

This Learning Short-take® is a bite sized learning package that aims to improve your skills and provide you with an opportunity for personal and professional development to achieve success in your role.

This Learning Short-take® combines self study with workplace activities in a unique learning system to keep you motivated and energized.
So let's get started!

Step 1:
What's inside?

- Learning Short-take®. This section contains all of the learning content and will guide you through the learning process.
- Learning Activities. You will be prompted to complete these as you read through.
- Learning Journal. This is a summary of your key learnings. Update it when prompted.
- Skill Development Action Plan. Learning is about taking action. This is your action plan where you'll plan how you will implement your learning.

Step 2:
Complete the Learning Short-take®

- Learning Short-takes® are best completed in a quiet environment that is free of distractions.
- Schedule time in your calendar to complete the Learning Short-take® and prioritize this time as an investment in your own professional development.
- Depending on the title, most participants complete the Learning Short-take® from 90 minutes to 2.5 hours.

Step 3:
Meet with your Manager/Coach

- Schedule a 30 minute meeting with your Manager or Coach.
- At this meeting share your completed Activities, Learning Journal and Skill Development Action Plan.
- Most importantly, discuss and agree on how you will implement your learning in your role.

GET VIP ACCESS TO YOUR MATERIALS

This Learning Short-take® includes an interactive activity book, associated tools and job aids, plus a bonus eBook.

1 Visit
https://www.catherinemattiske.com/books

2 Select your book

3 Click: **VIP ACCESS**

4 Enter the code: STM2022425

WELCOME

Strategic Training Management
Transforming the business of training

Strategic Training Management combines self-study with workplace activities to develop skills in effectively leading the training team to deliver organizational goals. It will guide you in evaluating your current approach to management of the training function and in developing new and innovative approaches for application in the workplace.

Learning and development managers are often highly competent trainers who have been promoted on their technical capability and have a history of success in designing and delivering learning outcomes. Apart from their knowledge of instructional design, training delivery, training administration, and training logistics, today's training manager must have skills in leadership, coaching, counseling, and resource planning. Furthermore, he or she must have a fundamental understanding of the broader business strategy and the impact and contribution of the Learning and Development function on organizational objectives.

By providing you with new, fresh methods in the various facets of learning and development management, **Strategic Training Management** should help you improve the success of your team.

Strategic Training Management includes the **Training Partnering Opportunities** and **Communication Plan**, provided as free downloadable tools.

1	Learning Short-take® > Start here
2	Learning Journal 81
3	Skill Development Action Plan 87
4	Quick Reference 93
5	Next Steps 113

"A mind is a fire to be kindled, not a vessel to be filled."

PLUTARCH

Now let's get started!

"*Leaders don't create followers,
they create more leaders.*"

TOM PETERS

Section 1

LEARNING SHORT-TAKE®

WHAT'S IN THIS LEARNING SHORT-TAKE®

Table of Contents

How to Complete Your Learning Short-take®	5
Activity Checklist	6
Learning Objectives	7
Let's Get Started	8
Part 1 - Expectations of the Training Function	9
Part 2 - The Changing Role of Training	15
Part 3 - The Training Management Function	27
Part 4 - Training Team - Roles & Responsibilities	43
Part 5 - Creating the Training Plan	47
Part 6 - Proactive Training Management	63
Part 7 - Communication	71

"You cannot teach a man anything. You can only help him discover it within himself."

GALILEO GALILEI

HOW TO COMPLETE YOUR LEARNING SHORT-TAKE®

1. **Reflect on your skills and abilities** managing the training team, and how well you use these skills to achieve success in training.

2. **Complete the Activities as directed.**

3. Highlight specific skill areas that you believe you could develop more. Add these to the **Learning Journal.** Add to your Learning Journal as you go.

4. When you have completed this Learning Short-take® **meet with your Manager/Coach.** In this meeting, you will jointly establish a personal **Skill Development Action Plan.**

5. **Subject to your coach's final review** and assessment, you will either sign off the module, or undertake further skill development as appropriate.

After you deliver a reprimand, it's important for people to understand that you still value them as human beings.

DON SHULA & KEN BLANCHARD

ACTIVITY CHECKLIST

During this Learning Short-take® you will be prompted to complete the following activities:

- Activity 1 -   Training Function Contribution   13
- Activity 2 -   Journey to SPC - Analysis   24
- Activity 3 -   Personal Influence Capability   30
- Activity 4 -   Personal Skill Analysis   34
- Activity 5a - Training Leader as Role Model   37
- Activity 5b - Role Modeling Behavior   38
- Activity 6 -   Time & Activity Analysis   41
- Activity 7a - Training SWOT Analysis   53
- Activity 7b - Current Activity Evaluation   54
- Activity 8 -   Measurement Analysis   60
- Activity 9 -   Team Action Plans   68
- Activity 10 - Partnering Opportunities 78
- Activity 11 - Build Communication Plan 79
- Learning Journal   81
- Skill Development Action Plan   87

"Organizations expect that learning from a training course will be transferred to the workplace."

CATHERINE MATTISKE

LEARNING OBJECTIVES

- Assess key business challenges against current training function contribution.
- Analyze each step of the Strategic Performance Consulting and Delivery Process cycles.
- Evaluate the role of Training Management and personal contribution.
- Assess personal Training Management skills and attributes as a role model.
- Calculate time and activity over the last four weeks.
- Use the Current Training Function Analysis tool.
- Complete a SWOT Analysis and current activity evaluation.
- Analyze Measurement processes.
- Map training team performance and create team action plans.
- List partnering opportunities, together with key stakeholders and build a communication plan.
- Create a Skill Development Action Plan.

"What sculpture is to a block of marble, education is to a human soul."

JOSEPH ADDISON

LET'S GET STARTED

Learning and Development Managers are often highly competent trainers who have been promoted on their technical capability and have a history of success in designing and delivering learning outcomes. Apart from their knowledge of instructional design, training delivery, training administration, and training logistics management, today's Training Manager must have skills in leadership, coaching, counseling, and resource planning. Furthermore, the Training Manager must have a fundamental understanding of the broader business strategy and the impact and contribution of the Training Manager function to organizational objectives.

During this Learning Short-take® the term *Training Manager* is used a generic role title. Depending on the organization any of the following titles may be in use: Training Director, Training Specialist, L&D Manager or others. In the context of this Learning Short-take®, Training Managers have the overall responsibility for learning and development function for a particular business unit/division within their organization or for the entire organization.

This Learning Short-take® combines self-study with workplace activities to develop skills in effectively leading the training team to deliver organizational goals. Participants will evaluate their current approach to management of the training function and develop new and innovative approaches for application in their role.

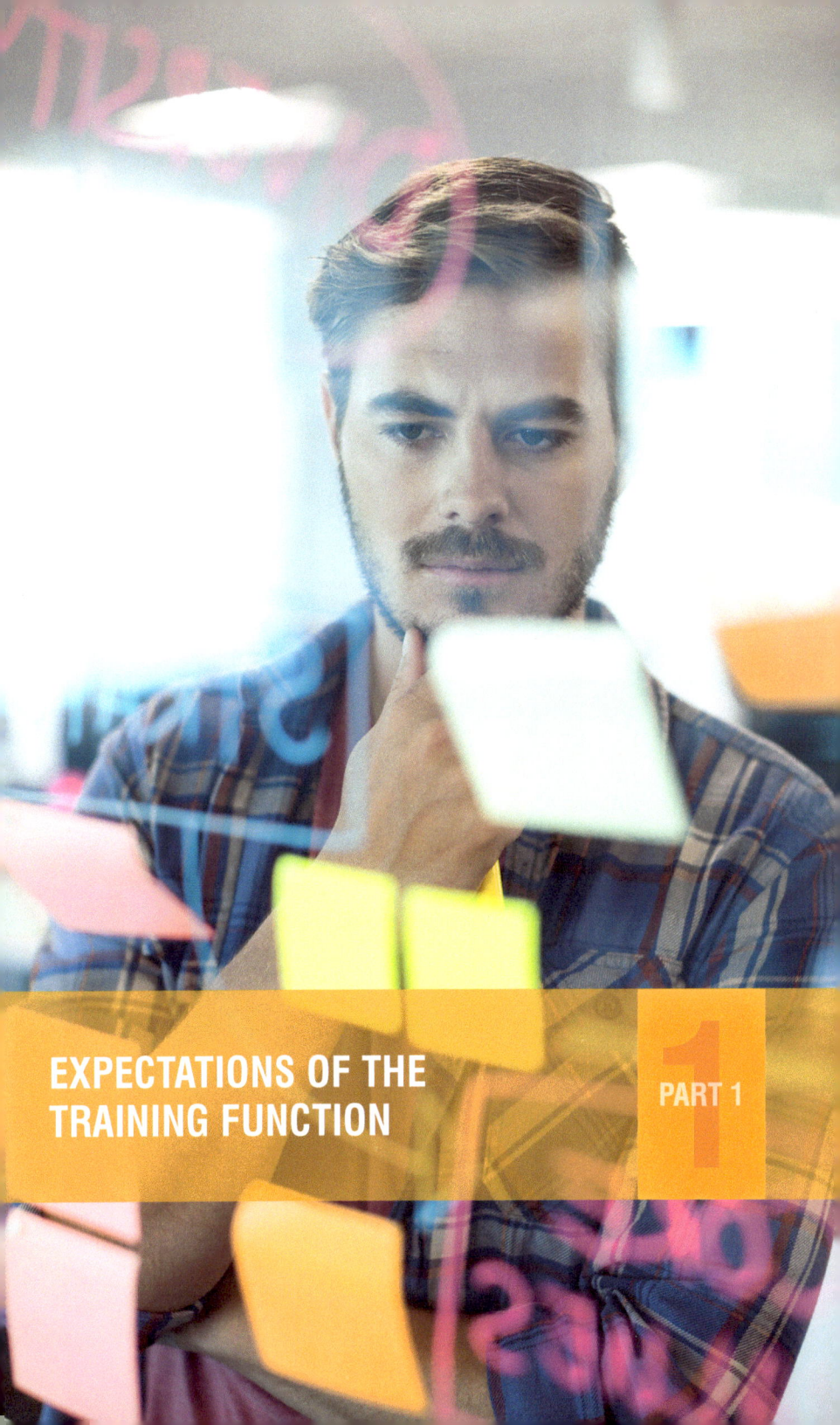

EXPECTATIONS OF THE TRAINING FUNCTION

PART 1

EXPECTATIONS OF THE TRAINING FUNCTION

"The current state of the training industry indicates that less than half of all Fortune 500 Companies even consider Training and Development in their strategic planning.

One of the main reasons is because the training department has not clarified or defined its own role and function within its organization. Best-in-class training departments have one key thing in common; they have clearly defined their role and purpose."

AMERICAN SOCIETY OF
TRAINING & DEVELOPMENT - JOURNAL 1999

This quote from 1999 still holds true today.

When executives ask for "proof" that the training function provides a positive Return on Investment (ROI), they are really looking for confidence in the training function to deliver business improvement. A common question amongst training professionals is that if senior managers were confident that training was meeting the needs of the business, would they demand a precisely measured value? Measurement is hard work and expensive. Many Training Managers state that when executives are already confident in the return on their training investment they do not expend resources "proving" that training is valuable but simply 'trust the process'. This somewhat unconventional way of measuring a business function, or in fact not measuring it, is often the way corporations manage their business.

Traditionally the training function was charged to develop and deliver training content, rather than to provide measurable business value. Furthermore, the training function often sets its priorities using fundamentally different performance criteria than that used by line managers. What today's business leaders expect is for their colleagues in training to think more like business owners. To do this effectively, training managers must accept that being good at one's craft is important only to the extent that it delivers value to the business.

Being good business people means understanding the customer's needs. It means consistently translating those needs into learning solutions. And it means ensuring flawless delivery of those solutions, day in and day out. Most of all, it means fitting cleanly into the business strategy and being able to credibly show one's customers - through measurement and through everyday business experience - that they are receiving unmistakable value. To do all those things well, training functions have gone through a fairly radical transformation and approach the management of learning and development activities as a business.

CEO Perceptions - 6 Business Challenges Faced by Organizations

Business Challenge	Modern Training Function Contribution
Financial Challenges - Reducing operating costs to increase production efficiency - Developing and implementing business strategies that result in profitable return - Maintaining operating profits in an increasingly competitive business environment	**Financial Challenges** - Understand the products of the company - Understand the company's business issues - Facilitate business model changes
Globalization Challenges - New employee skills to deal with a global economy - Cultural issues - New ways of doing business	**Globalization Challenges** - Understand the company's culture - Integrate culture into learning and development solutions
Recruiting Challenges - Attracting and retaining an appropriate number of qualified and competent staff - Filling key positions - Improving current employees	**Recruiting Challenges** - Increase workplace learning to attract new people to the organization - Participate in job seminars to educate the community about the organization
Customer Challenges - Ability to partner with customers - Helping customers understand how to shop and buy - Developing technology for greater customer satisfaction	**Customer Challenges** - Regularly consult with customers - Keep customers at the forefront of planned learning
Technology and Internet Challenges - Improving the use of technology to keep ahead of the competition - Gaining knowledge and employing those available technologies - Matching the latest technologies to customer requirements	**Technology and Internet Challenges** - Evaluate technological trends - Use technological trends to help change the business - Communicate trends to the organization
Corporate Knowledge Challenges - Shared understanding of the organization's objectives - Command of products and services to deepen customer relationships - Open communication and links between and among departments	**Corporate Knowledge Challenges** - Manage company wide transitions - Create a continual learning environment - Provide mentoring

Complete Activity # 1
Training Function Contribution

ACTIVITY 1: TRAINING FUNCTION CONTRIBUTION

Using the table below reflect on each challenge. For each, write current or planned projects that you or your training team is involved in that contribute to meeting this business challenge in your organization.

Business Challenge	Modern Training Function Contribution	Current Contribution
Financial Challenges		
• Reducing operating costs to increase production efficiency • Developing and implementing business strategies that result in profitable return • Maintaining operating profits in an increasingly competitive business environment	• Understand the products of the company • Understand the company's business issues • Facilitate business model changes	
Globalization Challenges		
• New employee skills to deal with a global economy • Cultural issues • New ways of doing business	• Understand the company's culture • Integrate culture into learning and development solutions	
Recruiting Challenges		
• Attracting and retaining an appropriate number of qualified and competent staff • Filling key positions • Improving current employees	• Increase workplace learning to attract new people to the organization • Participate in job fairs to educate the community about the organization	

ACTIVITY 1: CONTINUED

Business Challenge	Modern Training Function Contribution	Current Contribution
Customer Challenges		
• Ability to partner with customers • Helping customers understand how to shop and buy • Developing technology for greater customer satisfaction	• Regularly consult with customers • Keep customers at the forefront of planned learning	
Technology and Internet Challenges		
• Improving the use of technology to keep ahead of the competition • Gaining knowledge and employing those available technologies • Matching the latest technologies to customer requirements	• Evaluate technological trends • Use technological trends to help change the business • Communicate trends to the organization	
Corporate Knowledge Challenges		
• Shared understanding of the organization's objectives • Command of products and services to deepen customer relationships • Open communication and links between and among departments	• Manage company wide transitions • Create a continual learning environment • Provide mentoring	

Now update your Learning Journal (page 81)

THE CHANGING ROLE OF TRAINING

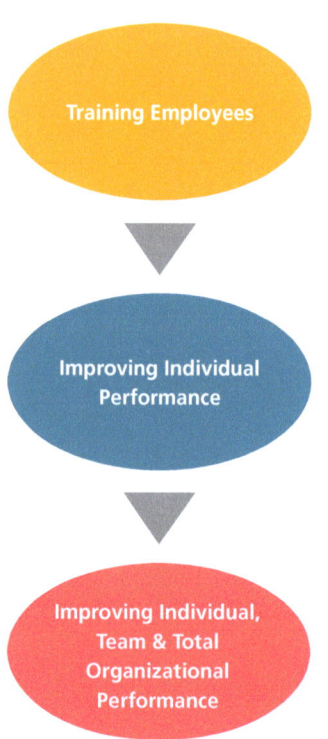

From 'Training' to 'Strategic Performance Consulting'

As a result of the shift in management expectations, the training function has evolved in recent years from a focus on **training employees** to **improve individual performance**, to a more comprehensive focus on **improving individual, team, and total organizational performance**.

Traditional training functions are under increasing pressure to make the transition from reactive service providers to proactive business partners, assisting the organization to achieve its objectives.

Training

Focuses on equipping individuals with the knowledge or skills they need to improve their performance to meet current job requirements. Training is essentially a short term learning intervention designed for immediate performance improvement.

It is generally implemented for a variety of purposes, such as orientation for new employees, developing employees for improved job performance, or cross-training, to prepare employees for critical business projects.

Trainers are involved primarily in face-to-face (In-person or virtual) and eLearning working with groups of people on courses, seminars or workshops. The trainer uses a range of methods for giving individuals the opportunity to acquire knowledge and skills for increasing effectiveness back at work. Trainers are responsible to the training function for providing a service to the rest of the organization by reacting to customer needs. Trainers also spend time in various administrative activities associated with planning and running a series of training courses.

"A leader leads by example, whether he intends to or not."

AUTHOR UNKNOWN

Strategic Performance Consulting

Strategic Performance Consulting is the integrated use of learning and other interventions for the purpose of improving performance, by addressing both individual and organizational needs that may or may not result in training. The Strategic Performance Consultant analyzes and responds to individual, team and organizational performance issues and has many customers or stakeholders both inside and outside of the organization. The performance consultant looks more closely at learning outcomes that are valued by the organization, typically measured in cost, quality, quantity, and timeliness.

The performance consultant works with a sponsoring client on a performance project. The consultant's role is to help the client accurately identify performance issues and to develop the appropriate intervention. Performance improvement interventions are aimed at the benefit of the whole organization, regardless of the client that the consultant is collaborating with on a particular project.

The sponsoring client may invite the services of the performance consultant, or the performance consultant may proactively influence a performance improvement project. Training may be just one part of the performance improvement project. The performance consultant may run a training program themselves, however is more likely to organize other internal or external resources to do this.

The performance consultant works closely with those who are formulating the long-term strategy and medium-term goals of the organization, and works at many levels in the organization simultaneously. He or she quantifies initiatives in data driven terms, gaining credibility with leaders and key stakeholders, and brings measurable results to the organization's bottom line.

Cycle Comparison

The Traditional Training Path

1. Identifying training needs
2. Setting training objectives
3. Selecting methods of validation and evaluation
4. Designing the training course
5. Running the training course
6. Carrying out validation and evaluation

The Modern Training and Performance Consulting Path

1. Gaining entry into the internal business
2. Agreeing a performance improvement contract
3. Data collection, analysis and diagnosis
4. Formulating proposals - learning and other interventions
5. Feedback to clients and decision to act
6. Implementation
7. Follow-up

From Training to Strategic Performance Consulting - Transition Model

Training		Strategic Performance Consulting
Narrower	**Organizational perspective**	Wider
Lesser	**Degree of influence**	Greater
Shorter	**Timescale of projects**	Longer
Single	**Levels of working**	Multiple
Reactive	**Orientation**	Proactive

What this Model means for the modern day Training Manager

As a result of the shift in thinking from 'Training' to 'Strategic Performance Consulting', today's Training and/or Organizational Development Managers have a far more strategic role to play in the business.

This means that they are not only responsible for providing a variety of learning interventions to the organization, they are accountable for improving overall business performance via a combination of strategically driven learning interventions.

Furthermore, they are responsible for leading and managing a group of training professionals to help them achieve this result.

Processes and Infrastructure of the Training Function

The Training Function must incorporate relevant processes and infrastructure. Core processes include:

- Training Leadership and Management
- Strategic Performance Consulting
- Delivery - Instructional Design & Training Delivery

Training Leadership & Management

In the Leadership and Management process the training function must **manage training activities effectively and efficiently**.

Effectiveness is defined as delivering training services that tangibly help the business to achieve its goals, and efficiency is making the service reliable and the true costs clear and acceptable to customers.

Effectiveness and efficiency should drive virtually everything one does as a leader or manager of the training function. The modern training manager has substantial operational management responsibilities.

It is not enough to be a great trainer or even to lead an organization of great trainers.

It is also critical to ensure that training is reliable, consistent, and successful.

Internal = Strategic Performance Consulting

The Strategic Performance Consult has responsibility for **identifying opportunities for the training function to provide value** - a responsibility that is fulfilled by working with, rather than selling to, the internal customer.

The Strategic Performance Consult may be assigned to the same set of customers (e.g. a particular business division) to coordinate logistics (facilities scheduling, materials production, instructor communication, billing, and the like) and to generally ensure smooth and efficient fulfilment of all training services. This person manages the relationship at every level.

Design & Delivery - Instructional Design & Training

Instructional Design

- Create the Program Outline
- Design the Learning Experience (Pre-, During & Post-Course inclusions)
- Produce 'ready to deliver' Learning Package

Training Administration

- Schedule Facilities, Trainers, Facilitators
- Participant Registration & Management
- Manage Logistics - Finances, Materials, Systems
- Manage Program Communications (Trainers, Participants, Managers)
- On-the-Day Logistics Assistance & Participant Support

Training Delivery

- Participant & Manager Communications (Pre-, During & Post-Course)
- Preparation, including Materials Walk-through
- Deploy & Facilitate the Learning Experience
- Provide Pre- and Post-Program Support
- Evaluation, Follow up & Feedback

Linking SPC with Delivery

Linking the Strategic Performance Consulting process with the Delivery process is crucial. Otherwise, the training delivered will not meet the needs identified by Strategic Performance Consultants and customers. Bringing these two functions together - especially when the processes are "owned" by corresponding specialist within the training function - is among the more complex challenges of the new training manager.

The following chart illustrates how the link between Strategic Performance Consulting and Delivery is best achieved.

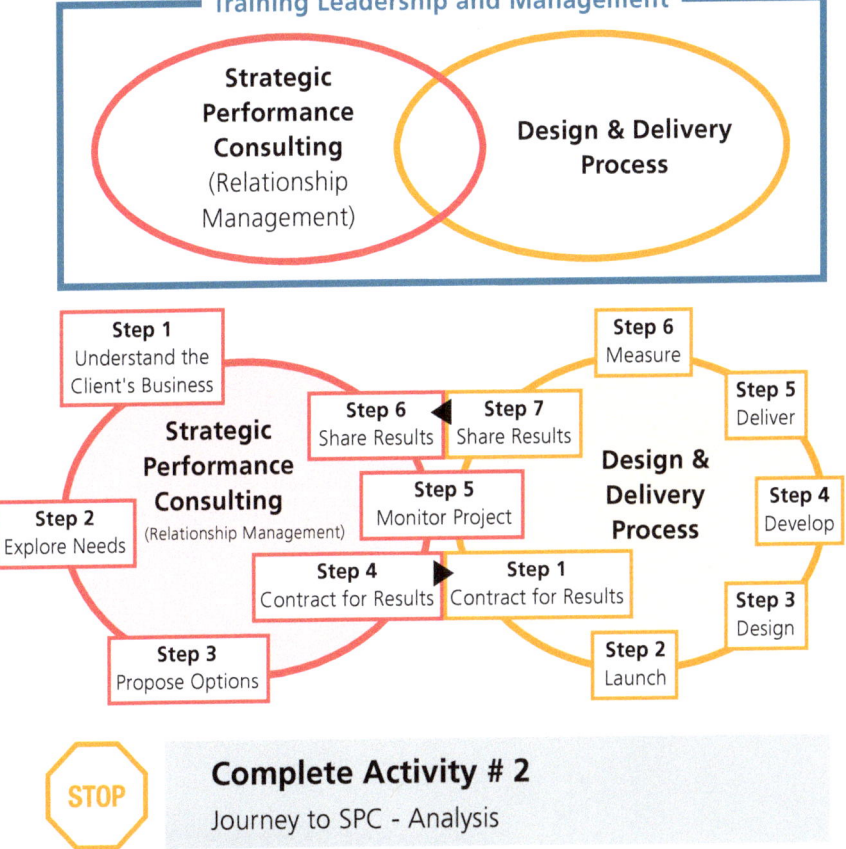

STOP

Complete Activity # 2
Journey to SPC - Analysis

ACTIVITY 2: JOURNEY TO SPC - ANALYSIS

Use this model to complete Activity 2.

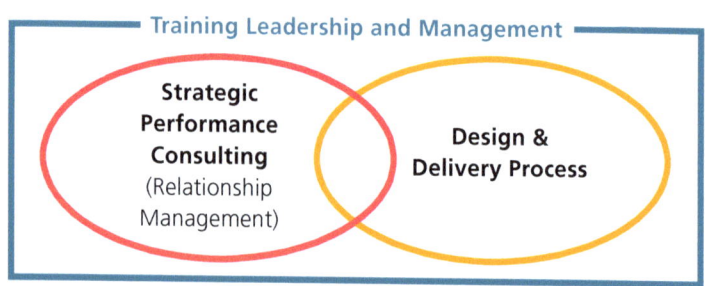

ACTIVITY 2: CONTINUED

For each of the steps of SPC and Training Delivery write current processes that are in place within the training function now together with any ideas for improvement and what the very first step of implementing your new idea/s might be.

Strategic Performance Consulting	Processes in Place	Ideas for Improvement	What is the First Step to Begin the Improvement?
Step 1 - Understand the Client's Business			
Step 2 - Explore Needs			
Step 3 - Propose Options			
Step 4 - Contract for Results			
Step 5 - Monitor Project			
Step 6 - Share Results			

Training Delivery	Processes in Place	Ideas for Improvement	What is the First Step to Begin the Improvement?
Step 1 - Contract for Results			
Step 2 - Launch			
Step 3 - Design			
Step 4 - Develop			
Step 5 - Deliver			
Step 6 - Measure Results			
Step 7 - Share Results			

Now update your Learning Journal (page 81)

"I am more afraid of an army of one hundred sheep led by a lion than an army of one hundred lions led by a sheep."

CHARLES MAURICE, PRINCE DE TALLEYRAND-PÉRIGORD

THE TRAINING MANAGEMENT FUNCTION

PART 3

THE TRAINING MANAGEMENT FUNCTION

Critical Skills

This part of the Learning Short-take® focuses on some of the most important skills for a Training Leader including:

1. Influencing Others
2. Business Acumen
3. Management Skills
4. Role Modeling
5. Personal Time & Priority Management

1 - Influencing Others

The successful Training Leader must proactively influence internal and external key stakeholders in order for their vision to be realized.

The seventh U.S. President, Andrew Jackson, once said, "one person with courage makes a majority." As a Training Leader it often takes enormous courage to influence. It's much easier to throw up our hands and walk away muttering, "I told them, but they just won't listen". The reason people don't listen often has a lot to do with the Training Leader's ability to influence. Your ability to influence has a lot to do with choice. In order to improve your influence you will have to change your choices and get to work on changing yourself to help change others.

Your ability to influence may be proactive:

- How do I sell my vision to the company when people are resisting change?
- How can I show senior leadership that training should be run like a business?
- How do I get my staff to produce greater results faster with less resources?
- How do I get people to listen when I speak at meetings?

Your ability to influence may also be reactive, when you are faced with obstacles such as:

- the staff you inherited
- the perception of training in your organization
- the difficult manager
- the state of the marketplace
- the limits of your role
- the company politics
- the perception of you by others (skill, career history, attitude etc)

Complete Activity # 3
Personal Influence Capability

ACTIVITY 3: PERSONAL INFLUENCE CAPABILITY

In order to increase your ability to influence it is useful to reflect on the components of successful influencing. Rate the following list to provide thought starters on how strong or weak each component is.

The following matrix will help determine your position with a person or group in a particular situation. This quick rating will allow you to form an objective and honest assessment of your position.

To complete the matrix:

1. Think of a person or group who you want to influence. Write these details at the top of the table
2. Note the situation.
3. For each of the components of influence, rate each 1 through 5.
4. Total each column
5. Multiply the total of each column by the number of that column
   (i.e. If you have 5 scores in Column 2 your total of column 2 will be 10)
6. Use the scoring grid below to help determine your course of action

Person/Group to influence: _____	1	2	3	4	5
Situation: _____	Exceptionally weak	Moderately weak	Average	Moderately strong	Exceptionally strong
my clarity around what a successful outcome would look like					
my understanding of their position and win (how they'll benefit?)					
my persuasion and communication skills					
my timing and the fit of my proposed action with the situation					
my tone and approach (will I increase or decrease defensiveness and conflict?)					
my genuine desire for a win/win outcome					

ACTIVITY 3: CONTINUED

Person/Group to influence:	1	2	3	4	5
Situation:	Exceptionally weak	Moderately weak	Average	Moderately strong	Exceptionally strong
my passion and commitment (including persistence)					
our levels of mutual trust					
the strength of our relationship					
how well I've covered the bases with other key influencers and built their support					
my appointed role, position, and authority					
Examples of where others have used the product/service/solution					
Key stakeholders who support me					
Previous history of success with this person/group					
Ability to ask for commitment					
Total multiplied by the column heading number					
Total (of all 5 columns)					

≥ 51: You are in a strong position to influence
30 - 50: Wait for a better time to influence or strengthen areas which will give you most benefit
≤ 29: Increase influence ability significantly, or think of another approach

Now update your Learning Journal (page 81)

"Sit down before fact as a little child, be prepared to give up every conceived notion, follow humbly wherever and whatever abysses nature leads, or you will learn nothing."

THOMAS HUXLEY

2 - Business Acumen

Business acumen is a concept pertaining to a person's knowledge and ability to make profitable business decisions. Originating within corporate learning and development circles, the term has seen a sharp rise in usage since the beginning of 2007.

The term "business acumen" can be broken down literally as a composite of its two component words: the Oxford English Dictionary defines **acumen** as "the ability to make good judgments and quick decisions". Given the standard definitions of **business** and what is "good" for business, a strictly literal definition would be "the ability to make profitable and quick business decisions."

The successful Training Leader will balance their vision of training and development within the organization with the available resources and the economic landscape of the organization while keeping all three in line with the overarching corporate vision and mission.

3 - Training Management Skills

Leadership and management are both important, but they seek to do different things. The successful Training Leader must be effective as a manager and as a leader. Most people talk as though leadership and management are the same thing. Fundamentally, they are very different.

Training Management

Managers manage things.

Management focuses on work. We manage work activities such as money, time, paperwork, materials, equipment, etc. Management focus more on:

Planning
Organizing
Directing
Controlling
Reviewing
Communicating
Coordinating
Resource use
Time management
Logistics and the supply chain
Finance and money management
Budgeting
Strategy
Decision Making
Problem Solving

Training Leadership

Leaders lead people.

Leadership has an essential focus on people and how they can be influenced. Leader's focus more on:

Vision
Inspiration
Persuasion
Motivation
Relationships
Team work
Listening

You can add to the list activities such as:

Counseling
Coaching
Teaching
Mentoring

Complete Activity # 4
Personal Skill Analysis

ACTIVITY 4: PERSONAL SKILL ANALYSIS

The first stage in any development process is to analyze where you are now. To help you assess your current situation complete the following 'self-development questionnaire'. Complete the questionnaire about yourself in relation to your present job. The objective is to help you think about your strengths and areas of development, and then use this analysis as a means of taking self-development action.

How do you rate your:

Importance – How important is this activity to my current job?
Competence – Which rating best describes your current level of skills, knowledge or ability?

	Importance ✔ A Very important to my current job B Of some importance C Of little or no importance			Competence ✔ 1. Outstanding ability in this area 2. Significant strength 3. About average 4. Areas of development that need improvement 5. Poor, considerable need for improvement				
	A	**B**	**C**	**1**	**2**	**3**	**4**	**5**
Planning • Awareness of management role • Future orientation • Planning techniques								
Organizing • Decision-making • Managing time and delegation • Recruiting and selecting • Training and development								
Directing • Leadership • Motivating • Giving feedback • Assertiveness								
Controlling • Budgeting • Problem solving • Appraising and disciplining								
Reviewing • Customer care • Managing change • Continuous Professional Development								
Communicating • Overcoming barriers by questioning & listening • Writing • Managing meetings								

ACTIVITY 4: CONTINUED

My major strength as a Training Manager is:

___

My major areas of development as a Training Manager are:

___

Analyze your previous responses. Prioritizing activities that you have marked as important (As or Bs) and where you have an opportunity for improvement (competence levels 3, 4 or 5) create a list of personal development ideas.

___

Now update your Learning Journal (page 81)

4 - Role Modeling

You can be a deliberate or unconscious role model, but either way, you **are** a role model.

- What you really value is evident from what you pay attention to and emphasize. These are your implied priorities.
- Your values become obvious from what you reward and punish.
- Your true cultural values are reflected in your actual behavior rather than your public statements.
- Your style/ personality/mindset manifests in organization and becomes institutionalized.

Complete Activity # 5a
Training Leader as Role Model

Complete Activity # 5b
Role Modeling Behavior

ACTIVITY 5A: TRAINING LEADER AS ROLE MODEL

1 - Read the following case study:

Axyium is a busy manufacturing company with a large training department. Felicity is the Chief Learning Officer (CLO) and has the responsibility of a multi-million dollar budget, 100 training employees and provides professional development to Axyium's 25,000 employees worldwide.

- Mark chuckled to himself. 2:10pm and Felicity is walking out of her office, laptop bag and purse in hand. As Felicity walked past his desk she remarked that she was going to a meeting with Todd in the Sales Department. Mark knew that Felicity was having the afternoon off as he'd heard her book an appointment at her hair salon for 3pm. He smiled as she walked out. 'Oh, that's just Felicity,' Mark thought '...Good for some that they can work part time on a huge salary! Me...I have to work company hours 8-5'.

- At 2:30pm Warrick, the CEO's assistant phoned Felicity to arrange a meeting. Felicity's phone went to voicemail. Warrick tried Felicity's cell phone - again voicemail. Warrick phoned Mark. Mark told Warrick that Felicity had left for the day and that she had told him that she was meeting with Todd.

- At 3pm Sam phoned Mark to arrange their gym workout for the following morning. Mark arranged it for 7am, then said to Sam 'No, how about 7:30am - that will get me to my desk by 9am'.

- The following day, Felicity had scheduled a 10am meeting with Mark regarding the worldwide training curriculum for the Sales department. Mark arrived at 10am, Felicity arrived hurriedly and unprepared at 10:10am. 'Nice hair', thought Mark. The meeting began at 10:20 after Felicity had prepared a cup of coffee for herself.

- The training curriculum project had been in progress for 7 weeks. The initial research had taken place, and Felicity had signed off on the plan of action. The next step in the project was to publish the curriculum and make it available to the sales force. Mark had prepared a draft training curriculum layout suitable for print and the company Learning Management System. Felicity gave Mark a look of disdain and pounced saying that Mark's efforts were poor and perhaps Mark should attend the company's Business Writing Skills program. Felicity showed Mark an example from another organization that was in line with her expectations.

- Felicity explained the timeline of the project and how it influenced other department projects and company wide projects. Mark hadn't been previously told about the deadline, the importance of this project and how it linked to others.

- Mark decided to take a break in the meeting and got himself a coffee. While he was out of the meeting room, Felicity called Mary into the meeting with Mark. She asked Mary to take over this part of the project and get the training curriculum published by the deadline. Felicity reiterated the project's importance and how strongly she agreed with the organizational commitment to the project's direction.

- Mark was silent. Mary gained Mark's agreement to assist her in the final stages of the project, despite Felicity's instruction for Mary to complete the task alone.

2 - Role Model Reflection: Using two different colors, highlight the positive and negative behaviors that Felicity exhibited.

Now update your Learning Journal (page 81)

ACTIVITY 5B: ROLE MODELING BEHAVIOR

It is important that during any process of change you act as a good ambassador for both your training department and organization.

Using your reflection notes from the case study in Activity 5a, list below the types of behaviors you think you should display and those you should avoid in your role.

Positive behavior - **use whenever possible**

Negative behavior - **avoid at all times**

Now update your Learning Journal (page 81)

5 - Personal Time & Priority Management

Balancing the Training Management Function

A series of training courses can be planned ahead in a logical manner, allowing time for preparation and other related activities. The workload is sequential, with a trainer running one course at a time, completing each assignment before starting the next.

However, a Training Manager has to let go of this sort of certainty in order to juggle several incomplete projects simultaneously. Timescales and commitments may need to be renegotiated as projects are extended, expanded into new areas or curtailed. Diary planning has to be flexible enough to cope with change and the unexpected. Above all, the Training Manger needs to be able to live permanently with 'work in progress' rather than the satisfaction of a series of finished assignments.

"Management is efficiency in climbing the ladder of success; leadership determines whether the ladder is leaning against the right wall."

STEPHEN R. COVEY

Time & Activity Breakdown

In any given month the work breakdown of the Training Manager may include some or all of the following:

- Responding to training requests from the business
- Proactively working with the business on learning and development opportunities
- Training (In-person or virtual)
- Instructional Design
- Administration
- Budgeting
- Reporting
- Coaching the Training Team
- Performance Coaching & Counselling
- Holding/attending meetings

Complete Activity # 6
Time & Activity Analysis

ACTIVITY 6: TIME & ACTIVITY ANALYSIS

Reflect on the past four work weeks. Use your calendar/schedule/diary for prompting information on how you spent your time. Record the number of hours on each. Total the hours. For each category, calculate the % of total.

Week beginning (insert date)	Week 4		Week 3		Week 2		Last week	
	Hours	%	Hours	%	Hours	%	Hours	%
• Responding to training requests from the business								
• Proactively working with the business on learning and development opportunities.								
• Training (In-person or virtual)								
• Instructional Design								
• Administration								
• Budgeting								
• Reporting								
• Coaching the Training Team								
• Performance Coaching & Counselling								
• Holding/attending meetings								
• Other _____								
• Other _____								
• General tasks								
Total	100%		100%		100%		100%	

ACTIVITY 6: CONTINUED

Reflect on your responses.

What does this indicate about the way you use your time?

In which areas would like to increase time?

How will you go about doing this?

In which areas would like to decrease time?

How will you go about doing this?

Now update your Learning Journal (page 81)

TRAINING TEAM - ROLES & RESPONSIBILITIES

PART 4

TRAINING TEAM - ROLES & RESPONSIBILITIES

"The only real mistake is the one from which we learn nothing."

JOHN POWELL

The key to delivering business improvement through the training function is **teamwork**. The performance of the training function depends on various specialists successfully blending their efforts over the course of a relatively complex operating process.

In the new learning and development environment, everyone has significant and specific responsibilities. It is important that everyone involved is accountable for a particular part of the process; thus avoiding confusion and inefficiency.

The roles, responsibilities and functions within the new Learning and Development environment often include the following:

Training & Development Manager	Assesses staff training requirements and creates programs to meet career development needs. Plans and administers training sessions, such as technical skills or employee relations issues. Supervises training staff. Managing conflict resolution, team building, or employee skill evaluations might be included in responsibilities. Assesses effectiveness of training. Could contract with vendors for special training services.
Performance Consultant	A role which is responsible for identifying and addressing the performance needs of people in an organization. The performance consultant determines performance gaps and the reasons for these gaps. He or she then provides services that assist in changing or improving performance. Interventions may or may not include training as well as other human resource related solutions that impact performance.
Instructional Designer	Writes and develops the learning intervention. This can be in-person or virtual training sessions, distance learning, e-learning, performance support tools or any other form of learning. The role includes researching and organizing the training content, creating the learning intervention, reviewing and updating existing learning interventions, writing, editing, proof-reading and other associated writing tasks. Also, instructional designers liaise with all other roles within the training function and at times with the client.
Training & Development Specialist	Plans, produces, and administers staff or management training sessions, for the organization. Delivers programs to develop employee skills and impart organization practices and policies by utilizing various learning methods. Technical skills or professional development training might be included in responsibilities. Investigates training resources for appropriate information, and suggests new topics.
Trainer / Facilitator	Provides training either in the classroom, virtually or onsite. This includes preparing materials prior to the class, managing and supporting pre-course work, teaching the class, and issuing, managing and supporting post-course work and associated activities. They have the responsibility for the entire learning process, and its environment, to ensure that the course meets its objectives and is measured and evaluated to understand how learning impacts business results.
Logistics Assistant	Manages the physical requirements of training. Ensures that all materials and associated items are prepared, packed and sent to the training venue, or hosted online in virtual sessions. Liaises with the Trainer to communicate project progress. May assist the Trainer during the training with the organizing of materials, and technical/systems support. After the training, unpacks, stores and refreshes materials.
Training Administrator	Schedules and manages all training administrative functions which may or may not include Logistics Assistant role combined in this role. Areas of responsibility are usually participant communication (nominations, confirmations etc), venue bookings, making travel arrangements for trainers and other administrative duties. Providing technical and systems support.

"

"Change will not come if we wait for some other person or some other time. We are the ones we've been waiting for. We are the change that we seek."

BARACK OBAMA

CREATING THE TRAINING PLAN

PART 5

CREATING THE TRAINING PLAN

"Leadership is action, not position."

DONALD H. MCGANNON

Research on high performing organizations is building a steadily growing base of evidence to show that organizations that train their staff better perform better. But training spend is not a good predictor of training impact. What seems to matter is whether training and development activity is linked with the knowledge, skills or behaviors most aligned with the business goals of the organization.

Many organizations do not have a single, visible plan for training; objectives and priorities may be more visible than 'plans'. Where plans do exist they may be multiple, covering parts of the organization (e.g. divisions or sites), particular workforce groups (e.g. managers) or specific types of training and development activity (e.g. centrally run courses). Training budgets are also often multiple and depending upon the organization global, but located centrally, and in line with the training function. These complex sets of training plans and budgets reflect the way training needs are identified in multiple locations and on different timescales.

Planning for training is also strongly influenced by the organization of the training and development function and the activities it provides. Some choices here are:

- whether the training and development function and the HR function are tightly integrated or more loosely linked, both at the center and in local units.

- whether the training function operates as a single centralized service communicating directly to the business or as a decentralized function, embedded in business units/divisions.

- how strongly key business functions control the content and delivery of development activities for their people across internal business boundaries.

- the degree of ownership which line managers manage plans for the training of their staff and training spend.

- how far and how fast the organization is shifting from the provision of courses to other learning methods of a more tailored and experiential kind (such as projects, secondments, coaching and mentoring, team development and organizational development).

Training Function - Key Result Areas

Key Result Areas of a typical training function may include

1. Creation and maintenance of a Training Business Plan.
2. Commissioning of external training.
3. Maintaining a database of approved training providers.
4. Maintaining a database of employee learning and development activity.
5. Producing learning and development reports.
6. Communicating with key stakeholders on the learning and development implications of organization-wide policy initiatives.
7. Devise and develop measures for evaluating the quality of training.
8. Publish reports on the up-take of training against budget for each division in the organization.
9. Ensure maintenance of instructional design standards across all internal and external programs.

Regularly Review Corporate Objectives

Training Managers can become so focused on the activities of the training function that they can lose sight of the broader goals of the organization. To stay focused on the bigger picture Training Managers should regularly review short-term, intermediate, and long-term goals and watch for indicators of a shift in direction.

Key areas for review might include:
- Annual reports
- Quarterly reports
- Press releases
- Internal and external speeches by key individuals
- Outside evaluators (financial community and auditors)
- Changes in organizational mission and vision statements
- Your leaders
- Other department heads

SWOT Analysis of the Training Function

A popular tool for analyzing the current state of the training function is a SWOT analysis. This approach provides an opportunity to think through business realities on which you build your learning and development plans. Strengths and Weaknesses focus on the internal organization while Opportunities and Threats focus on the external environment.

S **Strengths** - identify the positive features and people in your training function.

W **Weaknesses** - the problems, limitations and things that your people can't do.

O **Opportunities** - ways of exploiting strengths and developments you can take advantage of.

T **Threats** - problems caused by your weaknesses and threats from external forces.

"If you're walking down the right path and you're willing to keep walking, eventually you'll make progress."

BARACK OBAMA

Here are some useful questions to ask yourself as you compile a SWOT analysis for your training function:

Strengths
- What are we good at?
- What do we do best?
- What are our assets - finance, equipment, people, and location? Reputation, position in the industry?
- How do these compare with others?

Weaknesses
- What do we do less well?
- What do we do badly?
- What do we not do at all?
- Where do our competitor's assets surpass our own?
- Where else are we weak?

Opportunities
- What changes do we expect to see over the next twelve months that will present us with opportunities?
- What changes over the next five years will present us with opportunities?
- What long-term changes may present us with opportunities?

Threats
- What do other people have that is better than we have?
- Where are other people strong and we are weak?
- How easily can others enter our market?
- What changes in the external environment may cause a threat?

Complete Activity # 7a
Training SWOT Analysis

Complete Activity # 7b
Current Activity Evaluation

ACTIVITY 7A: TRAINING SWOT ANALYSIS

List your Training Department's Strengths, Weaknesses, Opportunities, and Threats:

Strengths
- What are we good at?
- What do we do best?
- What are our assets – finance, equipment, people, and location? Reputation, position in the industry?
- How do these compare with others?

Weaknesses
- What do we do less well?
- What do we do badly?
- What do we not do at all?
- Where do our competitor's assets surpass our own?
- Where else are we weak?

Opportunities
- What external changes do we expect to see over the next twelve months that will present us with opportunities?
- What external changes over the next five years will present us with opportunities?
- What long-term external changes may present us with opportunities?

Threats
- What do others people have that is better than we have?
- Where are others people strong and we are weak?
- How easily can others enter our market?
- What changes in the external environment may cause a threat?

Now update your Learning Journal (page 81)

ACTIVITY 7B: CURRENT ACTIVITY EVALUATION

Review your **SWOT Analysis**.

List those activities that make a real impact to the overall success of your training department and the organization.	Does this activity contribute towards us achieving the overall purpose of…	
	our training department	the whole organization
1		
2		
3		
4		
5		
6		
7		
8		
9		
10		

How will you manage the tasks that do not make a contribution?

Now update your Learning Journal (page 81)

Measuring Training

Ultimately you will want to demonstrate the bottom-line impact that the learning and development function has on the organization. Line managers will be keenly interested in the answers to these kinds of questions: "How has the product quality improved as a result of the learning interventions?", "How much have costs declined as a result?", and "What are the incremental sales of product?"

Evaluation & Measurement

In the early days of training, evaluation was used to identify the impact of a program, service or product. As the expectations on the learning and development function have increased, the focus of evaluation has shifted to identifying the impact of interventions on individual and organizational effectiveness. This level of evaluation has enabled the modern training manager to provide key stakeholders with information about how well learning and development interventions were implemented, and to determine how these can be made even more effective in the future. Learning evaluation should be undertaken Pre-, During, and Post-Course or Session.

"The only man who behaves sensibly is my tailor; he takes my measurements anew every time he sees me, while all the rest go on with their old measurements and expect me to fit them."

GEORGE BERNARD SHAW

Evaluation Tools

It is important for any organization to constantly evaluate the effectiveness of its corporate learning programs. Without evaluation, it can be difficult to determine whether or not employees are actually learning what you want them to learn. Furthermore, without evaluation, it can be difficult to justify continued investment in corporate learning initiatives.

Evaluation tools can and should be applied as pre-, during and post-course measures. Here are some examples:

Pre-Course Evaluation Tool

The pre-course evaluation tool provides a great opportunity to improve the participant experience, increase participant engagement and optimize participant retention of the material. It aims to gain insight into participant knowledge prior to the start of their training session; they can:

- assess their current understanding of the materials
- reflect on what they already know
- remain closely connected with their participant journey

Adult learning and development is an ever-evolving industry, and pre-course evaluations are designed to empower participant understanding from the outset through effective and tailored participant material.

> **FOR EXAMPLE: Pre-Course Evaluation – Initial Skills Assessment**
>
> The Activity # 4 - Personal Skill Analysis, from earlier in this Learning Short-take®, can be used as a Pre-Course evaluation.
>
> The activity is distributed to participants 7-10 days prior to the course start date, to complete as an interactive document or worksheet.
>
> This is designed to provide trainers with a valuable tool to help kick-off participant materials, gauge participant understanding of the material, identify potential areas of concern, allow participants to reflect, and help build an overall picture for adult learning that's tailored to the training objectives.
>
> A well-utilized initial skills assessment offers an ideal opportunity to ensure that participants have the foundational knowledge required to make maximum use of their time during training.

During Course Evaluation - Bridging Task

The Bridging Task, also known as an Integration Activity, is a powerful tool for participant success during training sessions. When placed between two training sessions or events, it:

- engages participant attention
- creates interest and enthusiasm for the next session
- helps build participant knowledge and understanding of the material

Through participant materials and activities designed specifically to aid and extend adult learning, Bridging Tasks provide an interactive, hands-on approach that can increase participant engagement with the content and ensure long term retention of material. They are an invaluable instrument in improving participants' commitment both to the current session, and those they may have missed before or will attend next.

FOR EXAMPLE: Bridging Task – Understanding Your Listening Style

In this example, developing individual listening skills is essential to encourage self-growth and professional development. The participant materials provided in the Listening Skills Program focus on providing an opportunity for participants to understand their personal listening style more deeply.

By asking participants to complete a Bridging Task between training sessions, individuals can access resources that help them develop valuable listening skills, impacting the way they interact with others.

Take a moment to identify your **Listening Style**:
- People-oriented
- Content-oriented
- Action-oriented
- Time-oriented

Once you have identified which of the styles best describes you, answer the following questions.

What style did you identify yourself as?

Why did you identify yourself as this style?

Based on your style, what are your current strengths as a listener?

Based on your style what are your current weaknesses as a listener?

Given the information about your style, how do you plan to improve your listening?
(List at least three behaviors)

1.
2.
3.

Post-Course Evaluation Tool – Skill Development Action Plan & Implementation

Training programs are the perfect opportunity for participants to acquire new skills and increase their knowledge. By providing participant materials such as a Skill Development Action Plan during the training, employees are equipped with a valuable resource to continue their learning journey in an organized and meaningful way.

Professional adult learning continues long after the training ends and by utilizing participant materials such as this action plan, participants can easily access materials from the initial training outside of their regular work environment to implement their learning at their own pace. Companies view organized action plans as an integral part of successful training because it:

- is a tangible reminder for employees (and their managers) about what has been learned in class
- allows them to engage with the material on a deeper level
- provides a measuring device for the training effectiveness and impact

This participant evaluation tool focuses on participant reaction toward training materials and adult learning outcomes by way of them identifying how they will transfer their learning to their job. It creates a feedback loop between participant and trainer, allowing the latter to adjust as needed in order to create an improved learning environment.

FOR EXAMPLE: Post-Course Evaluation – Skill Development Action Plan

Refer to your Skill Development Action Plan in this Learning Short-take® for a direct example.

The tool is distributed to participants as an integral part of their course materials and can be completed as an interactive tool, or handwritten worksheet.

1. Step one of this evaluation is asking participants to complete their Skill Development Action Plan at the end of the training program. They review their key learning and translate this into tangible actions.
2. Step two is following up with each participant on their progress as an essential part of the program. Depending on the circumstances, this may be done via the training team directly, or by engaging the participants' managers.

The training team is committed to connecting with each participant, providing support and seeing how they are progressing. Helping every participant reach their full potential and taking pride in supporting them as they carry out their action plans is a valuable part of the program and provides essential data to assess the program's impact.

In Conclusion

Completing participant evaluations before, during and after training, attending all training sessions, and receiving participant feedback, provides an effective method of adult learning for corporate training.

One of the aims of the evaluation is that participants feel empowered to focus on the key components of the training topic. They become curious through goal setting and increase self-awareness as a result of the program's design. All in all, evaluation throughout a training program aims to provide positive participant improvement in terms of confidence and skills growth.

From a corporate ROI (Return on Investment) perspective, including evaluations with a comprehensive support and feedback loop, helps Training Managers and their teams to assure the business that their employees are learning the necessary skills and tools to make meaningful connections with colleagues and customers alike.

Now complete Activity # 8
Measurement Analysis

ACTIVITY 8: MEASUREMENT ANALYSIS

Reflect on your current measurement practices and complete the following table:

Evaluation Level	Evaluation Description and Characteristics	What is the training function currently measuring at this level?	What could be implemented to strengthen the measurement at this level?
Pre-Course (Prior to start of training)	• Gain insight into participant knowledge and empower understanding from the outset		
During Course (During or in-between multiple sessions)	• Aid and extend learning, through hands-on approach and increased participant engagement		
Post-Course (After training transfer & implementation)	• Participants identify how they will transfer their learning to their job. Creates a feedback loop to adjust the learning environment		

Now update your Learning Journal (page 81)

"Everybody who is incapable of learning has taken to teaching."

OSCAR WILDE
"THE DECAY OF LYING"

"

"Leadership is lifting a person's vision to higher sights, the raising of a person's performance to a higher standard, the building of a personality beyond its normal limitations."

PETER DRUCKER

"

PART 6

PROACTIVE TRAINING MANAGEMENT

PROACTIVE TRAINING MANAGEMENT

Performance Distribution Curve of the Training Team

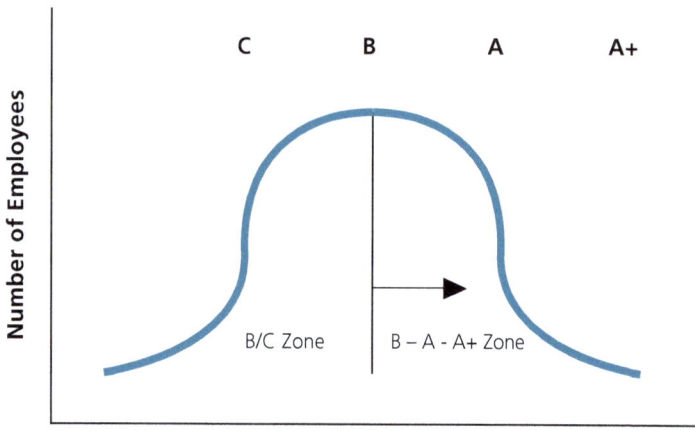

When looking at a typical training team, the chart shows a distribution of employees, ranged as A, B, and C players. There are approximately 20-25% A or top performers, about 50% B or middle of the road performers, and the rest, about 25%, C or low performers. Your training team may resemble this bell curve.

The question to be asked is: How much time is being spent on B and C players? In other words, what percentage of voice mails, e-mails, requests for assistance, or excuses about slips in the performance are from the B and C players? Probably too many.

The Training Manager 80/20 Rule

In a reactive world, Training Managers spend much of their time doing what they can to help their team achieve performance targets. However, often the people who request the largest amount of time and assistance are those who the Training Manager should not be spending time with. Training Managers should aim to spend 80% of their time with A employees, coaching them to become A+ employees.

- 'A' employees drive the learning and development culture. They rarely seek advice, and have the trust and respect of key stakeholders in the business.
- 'C' players, when given assistance, will always come back for more, which often means the same requests for help over and over.
- If you do not spend time with the 'A' players, they will most likely choose to leave the organization or move internally.

Focus on the top performers. It makes financial sense, it drives the culture, and it sends a clear message to the training team and to the rest of the organization. It is also more rewarding for the Training Manager.

Raising the Bar for Existing Training Team Members

As performance standards plateau in the training team, you must continue drive higher and higher levels of performance. Measure where each team member is, where you want them to be, how much time is available to improve their performance, and what their rate of learning is. Develop a performance improvement plan that is based on where you want them to be both in the short term and within 12 months.

Workplace Activities for developing the training team

1. **Coaching** - Have the a team member or a Manager act as a coach to one of their staff or colleagues.
2. **Delegation** - Remember this involves delegating a real part of your job not merely allocating a task.
3. **Project Work** - Particularly relevant when the individual needs to develop a skill which is not already part of their current job.
4. **Job Swaps** - Can be organized informally within your section to cover for sickness, leave etc.
5. **Secondments** - A more structured version of job swaps, usually for longer, often involving other departments or outside organizations.
6. **Deputizing** - Good practice for individuals in line for promotion or wanting to gain management skills.
7. **Shadowing** - Accompanying and observing a manager or other team member.
8. **Training** - Planning and running an in-house training event. Either reinforce or learn a new subject.
9. **Committee Membership** - A standing committee or special event. Gives an insight into procedures and politics.
10. **Hot Line** - Manning a phone response service, giving advice on unusual or difficult situation.
11. **Writing Reports** - Involves preliminary research into a topic. Opportunity to develop analytical and communication skills.

12. **Making Presentations** - A useful follow-up to report writing. Develops communication skills and opportunities to defend your case.
13. **External Representation** - Acting as an ambassador for the organization at an external event. Could also involve making a presentation.
14. **Product Champion** - The section's representative who will learn and be responsible for implementing a new product or procedure to your department.
15. **National Forums** - Representing the organization on a national body.
16. **Professional Representative** - Representing your specialty on internal or professional bodies.
17. **Trade Union Representative** - Acting for other members on local or national meetings.
18. **Study Visits** - Learning and reporting back about best practice in other organizations.
19. **Trade Exhibits** - Regional, national, specialist. Opportunity to update on new products or services.
20. **Vocational Qualification** - A work-related professional course combining a qualification with work-based projects.

Complete Activity # 9
Team Action Plans

ACTIVITY 9: TEAM ACTION PLANS

Write the name of each training team member where you think they are on the following diagram.

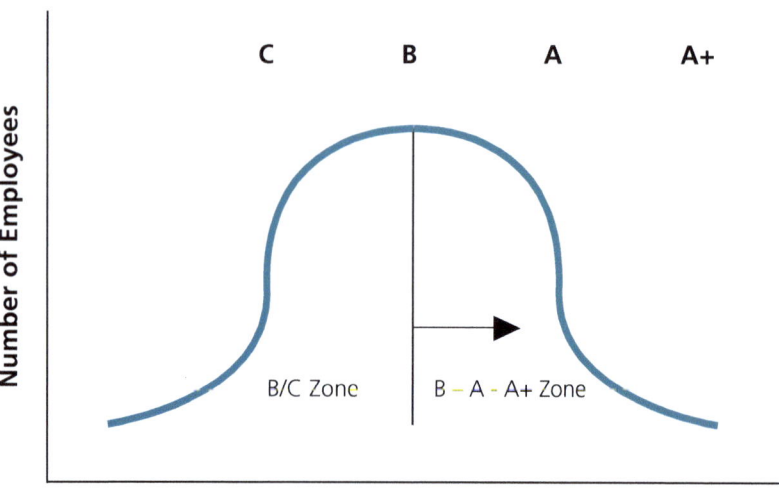

ACTIVITY 9: CONTINUED

For each team member list ways to advance them closer to or beyond A+

Name	Action Items
1.	
2.	
3.	
4.	
5.	
6.	
7.	
8.	
9.	
10.	
11.	
12.	
13.	
14.	
15.	
16.	
17.	
18.	
19.	
20.	

Now update your Learning Journal (page 81)

"I suppose that leadership at one time meant muscle; but today it means getting along with people."

INDIRA GANDHI

COMMUNICATION

"Setting an example is not the main means of influencing another, it is the only means."

ALBERT EINSTEIN

The importance of communication skills cannot be overstated when looking at the role of the Training Manager. Training Managers spend about 80% of their time communicating with others, continually managing interactions among people and groups. Communication permeates virtually every function of the training management role.

The Training Manager needs to be able to sit down and talk with people, understand what their issues are, and work collaboratively to determine the best intervention for addressing their needs. Communication skills are critical to developing trust and gaining credibility with internal clients, leaders and key stakeholders.

Identifying Stakeholders

Stakeholders can be internal, external, or both. The following list may be used to identify potential and actual stakeholders.

- The sponsor of the training department (sometimes called the client, customer, owner or funder)
- Other Senior Managers in the organization (Divisional HR Directors, Divisional Managers, Executive Committee, HR Department, IT)
- Suppliers, contractors, or vendors
- Professionals and other specialists who link with the training team
- Government agencies (local and central government) who regulate the training department's processes or deliverables
- The workforce who will use or be affected by the training department's outputs
- Special interest groups (charities, business associations, pressure groups) who also have an interest in the work and output of the training department.

"The problem with communication... is the illusion that it has been accomplished."

GEORGE BERNARD SHAW

CEO Perceptions - Importance of Communication Skills for Training Managers

"It begins with communication. Someone who doesn't possess or can't develop good communication skills in listening, speaking, and writing would not be effective in the Training Manager role."

"The ability to communicate is the number one attribute that Training Managers have to have. An individual who operates very effectively in a technical capacity, but who can't communicate well, will not get the job done."

"What's needed is strong engagement skills and someone who is very knowledgeable about their field. Only then will they be able to develop effective relationships with business leaders, built on trust and respect."

Specifically, the Training Manager needs to know how to:
- communicate effectively at all levels across the organization.
- articulate information, opinion and feelings.
- advocate on behalf of the organization and the individual.
- facilitate group processes.
- effectively communicate the interventions necessary to close a performance gap and achieve desired business results.
- select appropriate methods of communication to best get the message out and influence key stakeholders. Keep them informed and warn of potential problems.
- harness the energies of the training team.
- be honest and open to develop a relationship of mutual trust with other business leaders.
- seek involvement from key stakeholders to develop a sense of ownership and improved understanding of the learning and development function.

Communicating with Stakeholders

Here are some tips for managing your stakeholders:

- **Keep them informed.** Good communication helps solve problems, keeps the stakeholders informed and warns of possible problems.
- **Understand their needs.** Understand the requirements of the stakeholders and make sure they are met. Solutions to problems that are of no interest to them waste time and do not give any satisfaction.
- **Openness.** Be honest with the stakeholders and develop a relationship that encourages them to be honest. Good communications help.
- **State your needs.** Let the stakeholders know what your needs are and how they can be met.
- **Involvement.** Try, if practical, to let them be part of the team. Involve them in planning and team meetings. This encourages a sense of ownership and an improved understanding of the training department.
- **Negotiate.** Agreements with your stakeholders should be by negotiation to the satisfaction of all concerned. Both parties should walk away from the negotiating table convinced they have a good deal.

Guidelines for developing a Learning & Development Communication Plan

Step 1

Assemble the following:

- List of stakeholders and their roles, responsibilities, and physical locations.
- Any descriptions of communication requirements or related assumptions among stakeholders.
- Information about external reporting requirements (what do the public, the press, the government, and other outsiders need to know about the training function? How will they find out?).
- Information about technology available to support communication with the department (E.g. social media, e-mail, voice-mail, intranet, digital communication channels or groups, other digital media or apps).
- Information about typical communications methods for the industry or in your organization.

Step 2

What kind of information does each stakeholder need?

- List of information needed by each stakeholder.
- Typical information needed by stakeholders in similar departments.

Step 3

What technologies and methods of communication will provide stakeholders with all the information they need?

- List of appropriate communications methods and technologies.

Step 4

Create a training function communications plan that includes information about:

- Collection structure - How and by whom will information be gathered? What information will be gathered, and from whom?
- Distribution structure - To whom will information flow, and by what methods?
- Description of each type of information to be disseminated. What format, content, level of detail, conventions/definitions will be used?
- Schedules listing when each type of information will be produced.
- Methods for updating the communications plan in the future.

Complete Activity # 10
Partnering Opportunities

Complete Activity # 11
Build Communication Plan

ACTIVITY 10: PARTNERING OPPORTUNITIES

 Download the TPC Training Partnering Opportunities tool from the TPC website at **www.tpc.net.au/tools**

Activity using the TPC Training Partnering Opportunities

Download and complete the Training Partnering Opportunities Tool.

Now update your Learning Journal (page 81)

 Download the **TPC Training Partnering Opportunities** tool from https://www.catherinemattiske.com/books

ACTIVITY 11: BUILD COMMUNICATION PLAN

Download the TPC Communication Plan tool from the TPC website at **www.tpc.net.au/tools**

Activity using the TPC Communication Plan

Download and complete the Communication Plan Tool.

Now update your Learning Journal (page 81)

Download the **TPC Communication Plan** tool from htttps://www.catherinemattiske.com/books

"*Leadership is the art of getting someone else to do something you want done because he wants to do it.*"

DWIGHT EISENHOWER

Section 2
LEARNING JOURNAL

The Learning Journal is used throughout the process to record your key learnings, hot tips and things to remember.

Update your Learning Journal at anytime. Ensure you complete your Learning Journal after you finish each activity. Then turn back to the Learning Short-take® to continue your learning.

LEARNING JOURNAL

As you work through this Learning Short-take®, make detailed notes on this page of the lessons you have learned and any useful skill areas. For each lesson or refresher point think about how you could further develop this skill. Your coach will want to discuss these with you in your Skill Development Action Planning meeting.

*"…that is what learning is.
You suddenly understand something you've understood all your life, but in a new way."*
DORIS LESSING

"Act as though it were impossible to fail."
WINSTON CHURCHILL

> *"The wise do at once what the fool does later."*
> BALTASAR GRACIAN (1601-58), SPANISH JESUIT PRIEST AND AUTHOR.

Learning or Idea	Action to be taken	Result Expected

Learning Journal - continued

Learning or Idea	Action to be taken	Result Expected

"Anyone who stops learning is old, whether at twenty or eighty."
HENRY FORD

Learning or Idea	Action to be taken	Result Expected

*You gain strength, courage, and confidence
by every experience in which you really stop
to look fear in the face...
The danger lies in refusing to face the fear,
in not daring to come to grips with it...
You must make yourself succeed every time.
You must do the thing you think you cannot do."*

ELEANOR ROOSEVELT

Section 3

SKILL DEVELOPMENT ACTION PLAN

Your Skill Development Action Plan is the last Step in the process. After you have completed the Learning Short-take® and all Activities, update your Learning Journal, then complete this section.

SKILL DEVELOPMENT ACTION PLAN

This is the most important part of the program - your individual Skill Development Action Plan.

You need to complete this plan before meeting with your manager or prior to on-going coaching. You will discuss it in detail with your manager or coach as he or she will ensure that you have everything you need to complete the tasks and activities.

Once you have completed your **Skill Development Action Plan** schedule a meeting time with your manager or coach to review your plan. Take your Learning Short-take® and all other documentation received during the training course to this meeting.

Remember - you have committed to your **Skill Development Action Plan**, and need to make time to complete your tasks!

"The mind, once stretched by a new idea, never regains its original dimensions."

OLIVER WENDELL HOLMES

"Whatever you can do or dream you can - begin it. Boldness has genius, power and magic."

JOHANN WOLFGANG VON GOETHE

"Imagination is the eye of the soul."
JOSEPH JOUBERT (1754-1824)

Task or activity (Be specific)	Measure (this will help you to know you have achieved it)	Date (Be specific)
Reflect on your Learning Journal. Transfer action items that you can apply to your job. Ensure that you include some 'stretch goals' and also a blend of short, medium and long term goals.	Apart from you, who else is needed to assist you in achieving your goal.	Be specific. A general date such as 'Quarter 1', 'August', or 'by end of year' is vague and more likely to result in not achieving your target. Be specific – e.g. 22nd November.

IDEAS FOR DISCUSSION WITH MY MANAGER

Ideas

CONGRATULATIONS!

You've now completed this Learning Short-take®.

Meet with your Manager/Coach to discuss your
Skill Development Action Plan.

Further Reading

Cilliers, F., Herman, N., Adendorff, H., Vleuten, C. P., & Vleuten, C. P. (2012). A model of the pre-assessment learning effects of summative assessment in medical education. Advances in Health Sciences Education.

Korte, R. (2006). Training Implementation: Variations Affecting Delivery. Advances in Developing Human Resources.

McTighe, J., & O'Connor, K. (n.d.). Seven practices for effective learning. Educational Leadership,

"
"A leader takes people where they want to go. A great leader takes people where they don't necessarily want to go, but ought to be."

ROSALYNN CARTER

QUICK REFERENCE

This Quick Reference provides you with a summary of key concepts, models and reference material from Learning Short-takes®. We have also included some quotations to ponder.

Use this section as a quick reference to keep your learning active.

Quick Reference

The Training Function

Training functions have gone through a radical transformation and approach the management of learning and development activities as a business, which means:

- understanding the customer's needs
- consistently translating those needs into learning solutions
- ensuring flawless delivery of those solutions, day in and day out
- fitting cleanly into the business strategy
- being able to credibly show value through evaluation and business experience

6 Business Challenges Faced by Organizations

Business Challenge	Modern Training Function Contribution
Financial Challenges - Reducing operating costs to increase production efficiency - Developing and implementing business strategies that result in profitable return - Maintaining operating profits in an increasingly competitive business environment	**Financial Challenges** - Understand the products of the company - Understand the company's business issues - Facilitate business model changes
Globalization Challenges - New employee skills to deal with a global economy - Cultural issues - New ways of doing business	**Globalization Challenges** - Understand the company's culture - Integrate culture into learning and development solutions
Recruiting Challenges - Attracting and retaining an appropriate number of qualified and competent staff - Filling key positions - Improving current employees	**Recruiting Challenges** - Increase workplace learning to attract new people to the organization - Participate in job seminars to educate the community about the organization
Customer Challenges - Ability to partner with customers - Helping customers understand how to shop and buy - Developing technology for greater customer satisfaction	**Customer Challenges** - Regularly consult with customers - Keep customers at the forefront of planned learning
Technology and Internet Challenges - Improving the use of technology to keep ahead of the competition - Gaining knowledge and employing those available technologies - Matching the latest technologies to customer requirements	**Technology and Internet Challenges** - Evaluate technological trends - Use technological trends to help change the business - Communicate trends to the organization
Corporate Knowledge Challenges - Shared understanding of the organization's objectives - Command of products and services to deepen customer relationships - Open communication and links between and among departments	**Corporate Knowledge Challenges** - Manage company wide transitions - Create a continual learning environment - Provide mentoring

Quick Reference

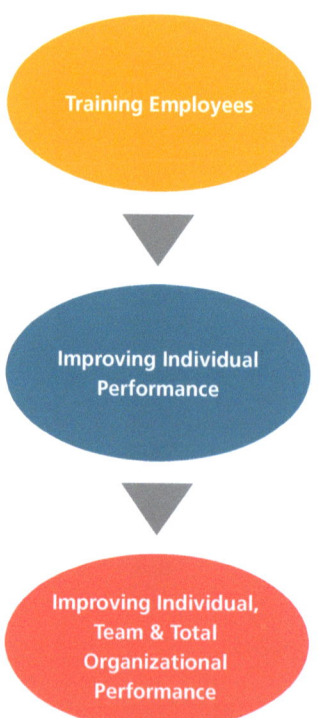

The Changing Role of Training

The training function has evolved to a more comprehensive focus on improving individual, team and total organizational performance.

Traditional training functions are under increasing pressure to make the transition from reactive service providers to proactive business partners, assisting the organization to achieve its objectives.

From Training to Strategic Performance Consulting – Transition Model

Training		Strategic Performance Consulting
Narrower	**Organizational perspective**	Wider
Lesser	**Degree of influence**	Greater
Shorter	**Timescale of projects**	Longer
Single	**Levels of working**	Multiple
Reactive	**Orientation**	Proactive

Quick Reference

Linking SPC with Delivery

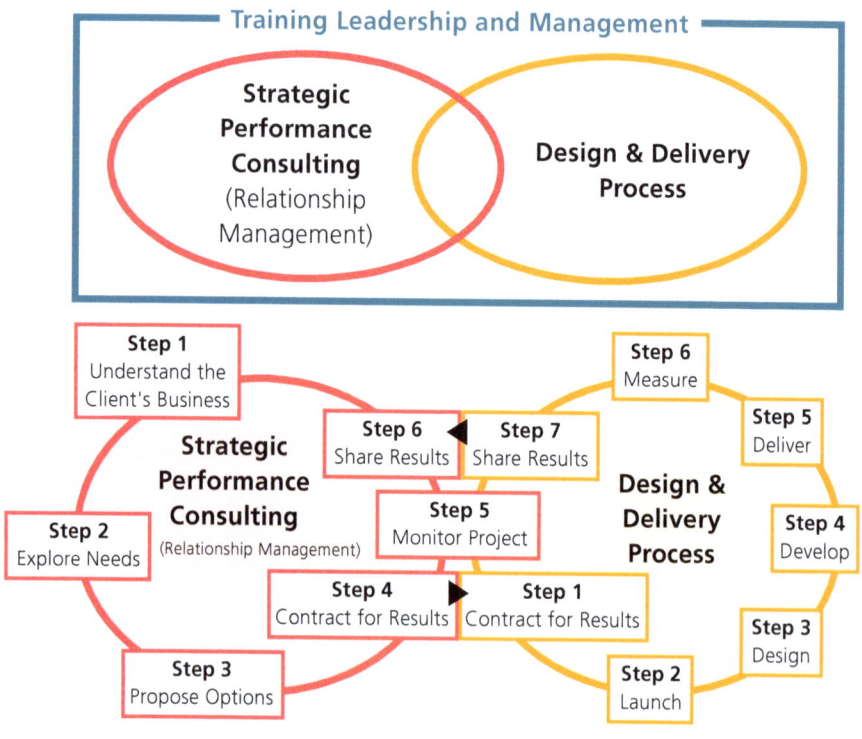

The Training Management Function – Critical Skills

The most important skills for a Training Leader include:

1. **Influencing Others**
2. **Business Acumen**
3. **Management Skills**
4. **Role Modeling**
5. **Personal Time & Priority Management**

Quick Reference

> **Management is efficiency in climbing the ladder of success; leadership determines whether the ladder is leaning against the right wall.**
>
> STEPHEN R. COVEY

Training Roles & Responsibilities

- **Training & Development Manager**
- **Performance Consultant**
- **Instructional Designer**
- **Training & Development Specialist**
- **Logistics Assistant**
- **Training Administrator**

Quick Reference

> **Change will not come if we wait for some other person or some other time. We are the ones we've been waiting for. We are the change that we seek.**

BARACK OBAMA

Training Function – Key Result Areas

Key Result Areas of a typical training function may include

1. Creation and maintenance of a Training Business Plan.
2. Commissioning of external training.
3. Maintaining a database of approved training providers.
4. Maintaining a database of employee learning and development activity.
5. Producing learning and development reports.
6. Communicating with key stakeholders on the learning and development implications of organization-wide policy initiatives.
7. Devise and develop measures for evaluating the quality of training.
8. Publish reports on the up-take of training against budget for each division in the organization.
9. Ensure maintenance of instructional design standards across all internal and external programs.

Quick Reference

SWOT Analysis

S **Strengths** - identify the positive features and people in your training function.

W **Weaknesses** - the problems, limitations and things that your people can't do.

O **Opportunities** - ways of exploiting strengths and developments you can take advantage of.

T **Threats** - problems caused by your weaknesses and threats from external forces.

Evaluation & Measurement

Evaluation Level	Timing in the Learning Process	Evaluation Description and Characteristics	Example
Pre-Course Evaluation Tool	Distributed in advance, prior to the start of the training.	To gain insight into participant knowledge and empower participant understanding from the outset through effective and tailored participant material.	Initial Skills Assessment
During Course Evaluation Tool	Provided during the training, for in-between two training sessions/events	To specifically aid and extend learning, and provide a hands-on approach that can increase participant engagement with the content and ensure long term retention of material.	Bridging Task
Post-Course Evaluation Tool	Provided towards the end of a session and utilized afterwards as an implementation activity	Focused on participant reaction toward training materials and adult learning outcomes by way of them identifying how they will transfer their learning to their job. It creates a feedback loop allowing adjustment to create an improved learning environment.	Skill Development Action Plan

Quick Reference

> **Leadership is lifting a person's vision to higher sights, the raising of a person's performance to a higher standard, the building of a personality beyond its normal limitations.**
>
> PETER DRUCKER

Performance Distribution Curve of the Training Team

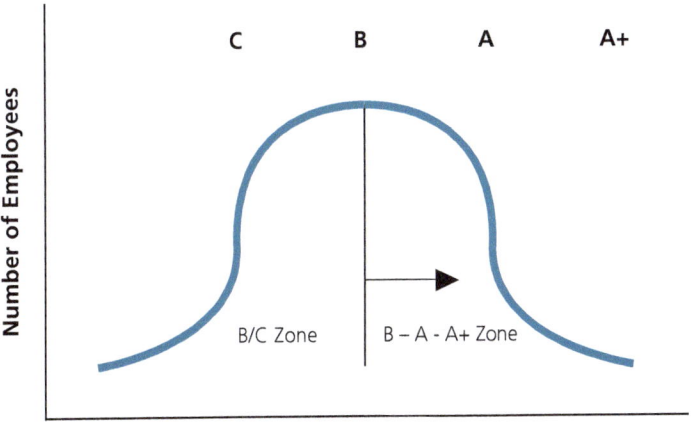

Quick Reference

Workplace Activities for Developing the Training Team

1. Coaching
2. Delegation
3. Project Work
4. Job Swaps
5. Secondments
6. Deputizing
7. Shadowing
8. Training
9. Committee Membership
10. Hot Line
11. Writing Reports
12. Making Presentations
13. External Representation
14. Product Champion
15. National Forums
16. Professional Representative
17. Trade Union Representative
18. Study Visits
19. Trade Exhibits
20. Vocational Qualification

Communicating with Stakeholders

- **Keep them informed.** Good communication helps solve problems, keeps the stakeholders informed and warns of possible problems.

- **Understand their needs.** Understand the requirements of the stakeholders and make sure they are met. Solutions to problems that are of no interest to them waste time and do not give any satisfaction.

- **Openness.** Be honest with the stakeholders and develop a relationship that encourages them to be honest. Good communications help.

- **State your needs.** Let the stakeholders know what your needs are and how they can be met.

- **Involvement.** Try, if practical, to let them be part of the team. Involve them in planning and team meetings. This encourages a sense of ownership and an improved understanding of the training department.

- **Negotiate.** Agreements with your stakeholders should be by negotiation to the satisfaction of all concerned. Both parties should walk away from the negotiating table convinced they have a good deal.

Quick Reference

Guidelines for Developing a Learning & Development Communication Plan

Step 1 – Assemble Key Information

- List of stakeholders
- Communication requirements or related assumptions among stakeholders
- External reporting requirements
- Technology available to support communication
- Typical communications methods for the industry/your organization

Step 2 - What kind of information does each stakeholder need?

- Information needed by each stakeholder
- Typical information needed by stakeholders in similar departments

Step 3 – Technologies & Methods of Communication

- Communications methods and technologies

Step 4 – Create a training function communications plan

- Collection structure
- Distribution structure
- Each type of information to be disseminated
- Schedules listing
- Methods for future plan updates

> **Leadership is the art of getting someone else to do something you want done because he wants to do it.**
>
> Dwight Eisenhower

> **Effective leadership is not about making speeches or being liked; leadership is defined by results not attributes.**

Peter Drucker

NEXT STEPS

Congratulations! You have now completed this Learning Short-take® title. The entire list of Learning Short-takes® can be found on the catherinemattiske.com website.

In this section we have suggested Learning Short-take® titles for you that will build your learning. You may order these Learning Short-takes® online at https://www.catherinemattiske.com/books or from your bookstores.

Successful Project Management
A Step-by-Step Toolkit for Project Success

Learning Short-take® Outline

Successful Project Management explores effective strategies to planning and implementing projects within your organization using proven Project Planning tools. You will learn the keys to successful project management by following a structured approach to project planning, implementation and review. By using a real workplace project, **Successful Project Management** strengthens your project management skills. It covers both the essential theory and practical skills for project excellence.

Project Management is a method and set of techniques based on planning, estimating and determining work activities to achieve a desired result on time, within budget and according to specification. During a project's life cycle, project management focuses on three basic parameters: quality, time and cost. A successfully managed project is one that is completed to specified quality, on or before the deadline, and within budget.

Successful Project Management includes the **Problem Summary Report, Project Evaluation Report, Project Plan, Project Status Report, Project Task List**, and the **Work Package Assignment**, provided as free downloadable tools.

Learning Objectives

- Build direction and standards when managing projects.
- Focus on your current projects, looking for improvement opportunities.
- Work through the Project Management Life Cycle.
- Use standard forms and tools.
- Create a Skill Development Action Plan.

Course Content

- Part 1: Project Management Fundamentals
- Part 2: The Project Lifecycle
- Part 3: Phase 1 - Define the Project
- Part 4: Phase 2 - Plan the Project
- Part 5: Phase 3 - Implement the Project
- Part 6: Phase 4 - Close the Project

Making Meetings Work
Getting the Most out of Meetings

Course Content

- Part 1: Types of Meetings
- Part 2: Why Meetings Fail
- Part 3: Solutions to Meeting Barriers
- Part 4: Planning the Meeting
- Part 5: Preparing the Agenda
- Part 6: Conducting the Meeting

Learning Short-take® Outline

Making Meetings Work combines self-study with realistic workplace activities to provide you with the key skills and techniques to make meetings work. Your meetings will become more focused, efficient, targeted and more likely to have a productive impact on the company's bottom-line. You will learn how to more effectively prepare, manage, facilitate and actively participate in meetings.

It is estimated that the average professional spends 61.5 hours per month in meetings, or two weeks every year. It is also estimated that at least 50% of this time is wasted in unproductive meeting activity. **Making Meetings Work** will provide you with the tools to help you save time and money.

Making Meetings Work includes the **Meeting Administration Checklist, Meeting Agenda** and **Meeting Minutes** provided as free downloadable tools.

Learning Objectives

- Evaluate your current level of meeting success.
- Identify the various types of meetings and explain key differences.
- Develop solutions to common meeting problems.
- Outline the steps for a successful meeting.
- Carry out meeting planning and preparation.
- Create a Skill Development Action Plan.

The Effective Leader
Skills and Tools for Inspired Leadership

Learning Short-take® Outline

The Effective Leader will guide managers and leaders at all levels towards maximizing your effectiveness as a leader in the workplace. By demystifying the key concepts of communication, team building, leadership styles, individual and team motivation, performance, and interpersonal skills, you will be better equipped for success in your leadership role.

The Effective Leader includes covers both the essential theory and practical skills for successful leadership of teams. Through a series of self-assessment and action learning activities you will identify the differences between management and leadership, write a vision and mission statements, and identify your natural leadership style.
The Effective Leader will illustrate how to use additional leadership styles and how to plan and lead effective team meetings.

Increased leadership skills moves individuals and teams to increased resilience in the face of change, enhanced performance and greater success!

The Effective Leader includes the **Meeting Planner, Meeting Agenda, Core Essentials of Compelling Vision & Mission Statements Job Aid,** and the **Leadership Styles Summary,** provided as free downloadable tools.

Learning Objectives

- Define the relationship between leadership and management.
- Understand the meaning of vision, mission and values.
- Know the role of leader as coach.
- Apply the theory of the functional and situational approaches to leadership.
- Work on the personal qualities of leadership and display the will to lead.
- Have a high regard for communication in the leadership process and develop the ability to communicate.
- List ways to influence motivation for each member of your team.
- Create a Skill Development Action Plan

Course Content

- Part 1: The Effective Leader
- Part 2: Management vs Leadership
- Part 3: Leadership Vision & Mission
- Part 4: Leadership Styles
- Part 5: Understanding Behavior
- Part 6: Leadership & Roles
- Part 7: Leading a Team

www.catherinemattiske.com

www.ingramcontent.com/pod-product-compliance
Lightning Source LLC
Chambersburg PA
CBHW042229090526
44587CB00001B/8